Copyright © 2025 Alex Daniell
All Rights Reserved.

All rights reserved. No part of this book may be reproduced or transmitted in any form or by any means electronic or mechanical including photocopying, recording, or by any information storage and retrieval system without permission in writing from the publisher or author.

Reincarnation by Alex Daniell

Aurora Books, an imprint of Eco-Justice Press, L.L.C.
www.ecojusticepress.com

ISBN 9978-1-945432-77-4

Reincarnation

Written by
Alex Daniell

Illustrated by
Lily Grey &
Jennifer Morrell

Andy McCormick was tired. He was an old man and he had lived a good life. His son had offered to drive him home from the funeral of his wife, down the long twisty Beaver Meadow road through the warm summer night, but he wanted to be alone.

"Well," he said to himself out loud, "I guess I've done it all pretty much right. Honestly speakin', don't really wanta go on without Margret. Wonder what I might wanta be in my next life?"

Andy was drifting. Letting ideas take him to different places in his mind. He was also drifting, as the road curved, across the yellow line.

Andy opened his eyes. There were green sparkling leaves all around. Leaves above him and leaves below him, moving. He had flown off the embankment and his car was upside down, falling through the air.

Andy didn't care. When he landed his soul drifted in a cloud of white mist out over the tranquil, moonlit stream.

Andy's soul held together an iridescent cloud, trying to form a coherent shape. It morphed into the form of a man and then a fish, a bird and then an otter.

It followed the wind over the water, and lifted above the silver corn fields when the stream turned, propelled towards a farm, drifting into the dark open door of a hayloft, settling into the body of a newborn kitten.

Oscar was a barn cat. He opened his eyes in a box of hay, staring at the immense menacing shadows stretching beyond infinity. His brothers and sisters were buried deep in their mother's fur, fighting for their teat, but not Oscar. He was studying the shadows.

Oscar was the smallest of his litter, but he was also the quickest and the smartest. He learned to stand on his hind legs, so that the farmer would squirt warm milk into his mouth from the cow's udder. He knew where the crunchies were hidden, and was always the first to eat when the bowl was filled. His right and left jab were almost invisible, and he could dematerialize and rematerialize in a silent orange streak.

Oscar never fought over food, or battled for the sunny spots in the barn windows. He never dreamed of overpowering his bigger brothers, or coveted his mother's attention. He was happy with what he received. He got what he wanted.

Oscar was different in other ways too. Oscar wondered. He wondered where the crunchies came from. He wondered about the noises of the tractor. He wondered why the pigs would disappear. But most of all he wondered about the lights of the farmhouse that glowed soft and warm across the snow. And he wondered about the beautiful cat that sat in the kitchen window.

In the springtime Oscar began to wander. He would wander up the side of the road, and down the edge of the stream, smelling and touching and feeling. He would sit very still in the grass and watch and listen and wonder. He had bright green eyes, with hairline slits in them that could close up so tightly in the daylight that his body would become invisible to the foxes and the raccoons and the birds. At night these slits would open up so wide that he could see the old spirits of the world, and the light of the stars burned as bright as the sun.

Oscar got bigger and wandered farther from the farm. He was a male cat, and he longed for love, the love of the orange cat in the farmhouse window. But the cat was never let out, and there was a huge barking dog chained in the yard, so he couldn't get near. Oscar longed for the love of his mother, but she had another litter, and no longer cared. Oscar longed for the companionship of his brothers and sisters, but they were always fighting, and he was scared. Oscar was not a hunter. He loved to stalk, but he did not like to kill, so he always went back for his crunchies at the farm.

Not far below the farm the valley opened up into a little meadow with a white house and a red barn. Oscar liked to go down there at night, and sit in the woods looking down on the meadow. A man and a woman lived in the house. They danced and sang and cooked delicious meals in the light of the fireplace in the kitchen. They slept out on the deck and watched, along with Oscar, the fireflies in the mist.

Sometimes Oscar would stay all night in the valley. After the man and woman had fallen asleep, their breath rising as mist in the cool moist air, Oscar would sneak chicken bones from the compost pile and crack them on a rock by the waterfall, where no one could hear. There were spirits in the moonlit mist, shadows of horses and dogs and children playing on the lawn, when the house was small and the barn was bigger. There were glowing embers, and the distant clanging of a metal forge. There was a big garden. Pigs and chickens roamed the barnyard.

One morning Oscar was late in getting back to the farm. All the crunchies were gone. He waited around all day and in the evening he had to fight with his brothers and sisters to get any food at all. When the sun fell he made his way back to the house in the valley. The man and the woman were walking up the road carrying a beam of light.

"Look, a little cat, said the man. He made a trilling sound just like momma cat. Oscar trilled back.

Oscar lived with the man and the woman in the white house in the meadow. It was scary at first, with the whirr of the refrigerator and the rumble of the furnace and the slippery tables and chairs. But they fed him all the crunchies he wanted, and he learned how to stay out from underfoot. They built him a cat door.

When the snows came Oscar slept with the man and the woman, at the foot of the bed. He called them to breakfast in the morning and to the bedroom at night. He led them on the game of chase, and the game of finger tag on the railing of the stairs. He would do yoga with the woman in the morning, and get up with the man to study in the middle of the night. He was very happy.

But he was also restless. Sometimes, watching the man bent over his desk, lost in his mental travels, he remembered being a man bent over a desk, dreaming of distant lands. Oscar could not leave the house, as the snow was piled four feet deep against his cat door. He was trapped with the old spirits of the night, the farmer who drank and then yelled, the children who cried. When it became too much for him he would yowl in the night. Then they would lock him in the spare bedroom.

One night, after a blizzard, Oscar could stand it no longer. The path from his cat door to the road was shoveled, and under the full moon he made his escape. With his orange fur puffed out, and his white feet padding on the freshly plowed road, he opened his eyes until he was invisible under the blinding moon. A light breeze blew crystals into the air, forming a veil, a ground on the canvas of the spirit world, into which he could see. Green hills emerged through the forest- a team of oxen drawing a wagon up the road towards him.

Oscar's feet burned in the snow, but it was of no consequence. There were silver flowers in the fields and flickering butterflies. He moved the blood to his feet, and to his ears, and made his way back to the farm, where he could watch the beautiful orange cat in the window. She called to him, and he called back to her. He bundled himself among snow and leaves under a log, burrowing deep. He could hear the stars crackling in the sky. In the morning he made his way up the window.

He looked into the eyes of the orange cat and she looked into his and suddenly Oscar the cat and Adam the man knew who she was. She was Margret.

So they scratched at the bottom of the window until it opened enough for Margret to squeeze through, and they made their escape to the little meadow with the white house and the red barn, where they lived with the man and the woman.

www.ingramcontent.com/pod-product-compliance
Lightning Source LLC
Chambersburg PA
CBRC091726070526
44586CB00008B/90